By Air, Sea, and Land
Trucks

Paul Stickland

W9-ARX-663

WATERBIRD BOOKS
Columbus, Ohio

Flatbed Truck

Flatbed trucks carry their loads on large, flat areas called *beds*. This flatbed is carrying pipes to a place where a building is being built.

This flatbed truck is on its way to pick up a load.

More About Flatbed Trucks

Flatbed trucks are easy to load and unload. The bed of the truck has low sides to hold the load in place.

Flatbed trucks have powerful engines. The engine
helps the truck pull heavy loads.

Construction Truck

This is a truck used for constructing buildings.

This special crane is moving a load of bricks.

More About Construction Trucks

The truck's strong crane makes loading and unloading materials easy. The crane is powered by the truck's engine.

The driver uses a lever to steer the crane. He can use the crane to put loads exactly where he wants them to go.

This **motortruck** has broken down.

Tow Truck

A **tow truck** will tow it to a garage.

More About Motortrucks

The truck's cab tilts forward so that a mechanic can repair the engine. A mechanic carries a toolbox full of special tools. Mechanics must know how to repair all different kinds of engines.

More About Tow Trucks

A tow truck pulls cars and trucks that have broken down.
It tows cars and trucks with a special hook.

Tanker Truck

This **tanker truck** carries gasoline to gas stations.

Trucks can get gasoline from a pump at the gas station.

More About Tanker Trucks

A tanker truck carries gasoline or other liquids in its tank. The gasoline is then pumped into huge tanks under the ground.

Trucks can pull heavy loads. They need large tanks to carry the gas they need to travel long distances.

Semitrucks

Semitrucks travel long distances.

They carry products to stores so people can buy them.

More About Semitrucks

Semitruck drivers are called *truckers*. Refrigerated semitrucks can carry fresh food long distances.

Most semitrucks have 18 wheels. They have
special brakes called *air brakes*. Most trucks even
have small beds so truckers can sleep at night.

What Did You Learn?

What did the driver of this truck forget to do with the load?

What type of truck is this?

Why do trucks need large gas tanks?

This is a dump truck. How might this truck help construction workers?

What is the driver of this truck called?

How many wheels do most semitrucks have?

The driver forgot to strap down the load so that it will not fall off and cause an accident.

Dump trucks can carry large loads that construction workers could not carry themselves.

This is a flatbed truck. It has a large, flat bed for carrying cargo.

The driver of this truck is called a *trucker*. He or she spends a great deal of time behind the wheel of a truck.

Trucks use a lot of fuel. They need large tanks to travel long distances.

Most semitrucks have eighteen wheels, two wheels under the cab and sixteen under the trailer.

**School Specialty
Children's Publishing**

Copyright © Paul Stickland 1992, 2004
Designed by Douglas Martin.

This edition published in the United States of America in 2004
by Waterbird Books,
an imprint of School Specialty Children's Publishing,
a member of the School Specialty Family.
8720 Orion Place, Columbus, OH 43240-2111
www.ChildrensSpecialty.com

Library of Congress Cataloging-in-Publication is on file with the publisher.

ISBN 0-7696-3379-X
Printed in China.
1 2 3 4 5 6 7 8 MP 08 07 06 05 04